THE PONY EXPRESS

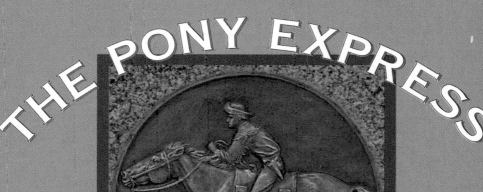

TRUE BOOK®
by
Elaine Landau

Children's Press®
A Division of Scholastic Inc.

New York Toronto London Auckland Sydney
Mexico City New Delhi Hong Kong
Danbury, Connecticut

Horseshoes and tools at an original Pony Express station

Content Consultant
Jacqueline Lewin
Curator of History
St. Joseph Museums, Inc.
Pony Express National Museum

Reading Consultant
Dr. Cecilia Minden-Cupp
Former Director, Language
and Literacy Program
Harvard Graduate School
of Education

Author's Dedication
For Carol, Karen, and Krista

The illustration on the cover shows a Pony Express rider on his route. The photograph on the title page is a monument placed by the American Pioneer Trails Association at the Gothenburg Pony Express Station in Nebraska.

Library of Congress Cataloging-in-Publication Data
Landau, Elaine.
    The Pony Express / by Elaine Landau.
        p. cm. — (A True Book)
    Includes bibliographical references and index.
    ISBN 0-516-25873-7 (lib. bdg.)   0-516-27905-X (pbk.)
    1. Pony express—History—Juvenile literature. 2. Express service—United States—History—19th century—Juvenile literature. 3. Postal service—United States—History—19th century—Juvenile literature. I. Title.
HE6375.P65L36 2006
383'.143'0973—dc22   2005020406

Contents

Delivering the Mail   5

A Wild Ride   18

Carrying On   30

Looking Back   38

To Find Out More   44

Important Words   46

Index   47

Meet the Author   48

This poster from 1861 advertises a new mail service called the Pony Express.

Delivering the Mail

MEN WANTED!
TEN OR A DOZEN MEN, FAMILIAR WITH
THE MANAGEMENT OF HORSES, AS
HOSTLERS OR RIDERS ON THE
OVERLAND EXPRESS ROUTE VIA
SALT LAKE CITY. WAGES $50 PER
MONTH AND [ROOM AND BOARD].

This help-wanted ad appeared in
a California newspaper nearly

150 years ago. The company that placed the ad wanted to hire a band of young riders for an important job. They were to carry mail on horseback between St. Joseph, Missouri, and Sacramento, California, at record speed.

These young men would have to ride through the wilderness of a still unsettled **frontier.** Blizzards or baking summer heat could not stop them. They were to be the first

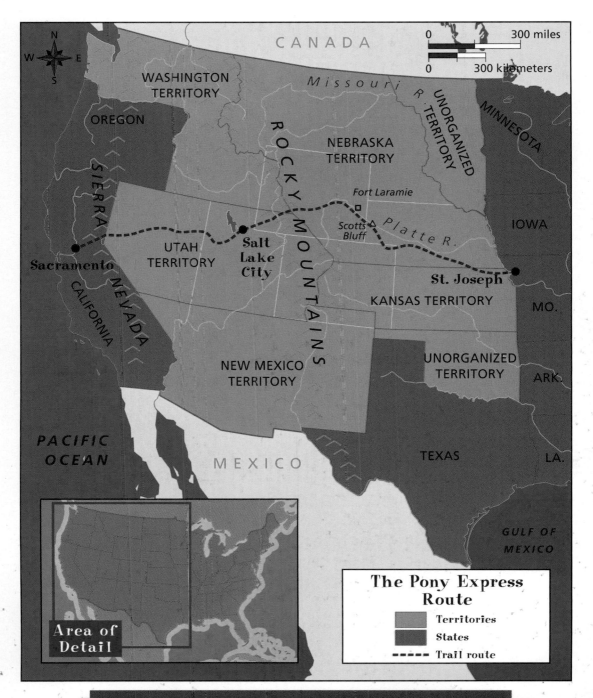

A map of the Pony Express, which ran from April 3, 1860, to October 24, 1861

riders for a speedy new mail delivery service called the **Pony Express.**

Today, you can send a letter across the country in just a few days. You can contact someone even faster using the telephone or e-mail. Back in 1860, things were very different. It was extremely hard for the half a million people who lived in the West to stay in touch with those in the East. This was largely because of poor mail service.

This view shows Red Rock Canyon in Wyoming. Pony Express riders rode their horses through this canyon.

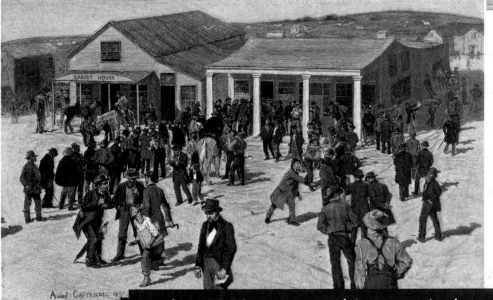

In the 1850s, steamships carried mail from New York to Panama (top). Then the mail traveled by land and ship to San Francisco, where people lined up to collect it (bottom).

At that time, mail traveled from one side of the country to the other by sea or land. Unfortunately, both **routes** were slow. With the sea route, the mail was carried by **steamship** from New York to Panama. From there, it was taken by canoe and mule pack. Then the mail was loaded onto another ship heading for San Francisco, California. It took three weeks to a month to get a letter that way.

The land route wasn't much faster. **Stagecoaches** carried mail across the country. They traveled slowly over the often rocky and uneven land. It still took about twenty-one days to get a letter by stagecoach. It wasn't possible to use the railroad or the **telegraph** because both went only as far as St. Joseph, Missouri.

The Pony Express was run by the Central Overland California and Pikes Peak

It often took weeks for stagecoaches to transport letters and packages.

Express Company (COC & PP). If the Pony Express succeeded, the company might earn a million dollar contract from the U.S. government for the country's general mail delivery.

The central route that the Pony Express riders used was the same route the company planned to use for regular mail delivery. The route ran through today's states of Kansas, Nebraska, Colorado, Wyoming, Utah, Nevada, and California.

Most Americans didn't think mail delivery over the central route during winter was possible. The Pony Express set out to prove them wrong.

While the central route was the shortest cross-country mail route, people doubted that it could be traveled year-round. They feared that severe winter weather would stop the mail.

Johnny Fry was the first Pony Express rider out of St. Joseph, Missouri.

A U.S. flag flies from the stables of the Pony Express station in St. Joseph.

The COC & PP started the Pony Express and worked to prove the doubters wrong. They hoped to show the nation that nothing could stop the mail. The first run began on April 3, 1860.

A Wild Ride

Two things could honestly be said about the Pony Express. The job was often dangerous, and it was rarely boring. Speed was important to these daring young men and their employer. Hard work and energy were important, too. Everything

A horseman takes part in a reenactment of the ten-day delivery rides, run by the National Pony Express Association.

possible was done to quicken a rider's journey.

Pony Express riders rode both day and night. Two riders always took to the trail. One traveled east, and the other traveled west. Sometimes there were more than two riders on the trail at once.

A series of **relay stations** were established along the route. Every 10 to 15 miles (16 to 24 kilometers), a Pony Express rider stopped at a relay

Pony Express riders changed horses at stops called relay stations.

station to exchange his tired horse for a rested one.

About every 75 miles (121 km), a new rider took over the route. By then, the original rider had been on five to eight different horses. Horses usually traveled about 10 miles (16 km) an hour.

A rider rarely stayed at a relay station for more than a few minutes. If he had made good time, he might have a quick lunch there. But most

During their run, the riders for the Pony Express had little time to rest.

riders just grabbed something
to eat while in the saddle.
A lot of planning, money,
and effort went into starting

This building is a replica of the Simpson Springs Station in Utah.

the Pony Express. The COC & PP set up about 153 stations and purchased more than 400 horses. The company bought the healthiest, fastest, and toughest horses it could find.

More than eighty riders were hired at any one time. Most riders were in their late teens and early twenties. It has been said that the youngest rider was just eleven years old, while the oldest was in his forties. Riders had to be slim so as not to add extra weight to the horse's load. Most weighed about 120 pounds (55 kilograms) or less.

Riders for the Pony Express also had to be of good character. They were required to swear their loyalty to the company. They had to promise not to fight, curse, or drink alcohol. The company often gave riders a small Bible and expected them to live by its teachings.

These young men had to cover a distance of nearly 2,000 miles (3,218 km) in just ten days in the summer.

These three men rode on the Utah stretch of the Pony Express trail.

Winter deliveries took between twelve and sixteen days. Riders carried only very small parcels and letters written on light paper, but

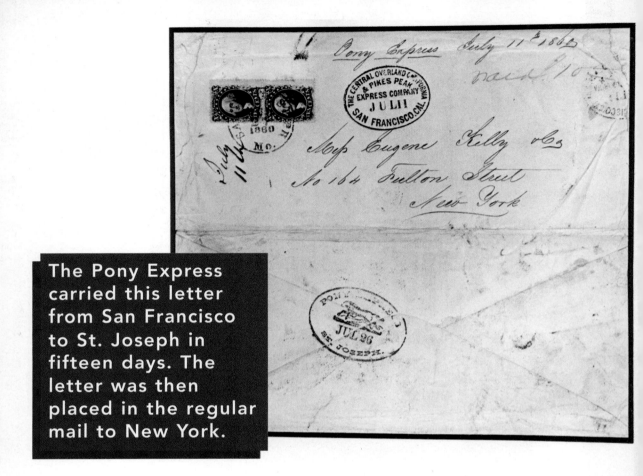

The Pony Express carried this letter from San Francisco to St. Joseph in fifteen days. The letter was then placed in the regular mail to New York.

they still had to push themselves and their horses to the limit. They had to meet the tight deadlines set by the company.

A Special Saddlebag

Today, some letter carriers travel with canvas bags or carts filled with mail. Pony Express riders carried letters in a leather saddlebag known as a mochila. *Mochila* (pronounced mo-CHEE-la) is the Spanish word for "knapsack." Mochilas were placed directly over the saddle, where the rider's weight kept it from slipping. The four corners of the mochila had pockets filled with letters. A full mochila could hold nearly 20 pounds (9 kg) of mail. During its entire time of service, the Pony Express lost only one mochila.

A Pony Express mochila

Carrying On

Pony Express riders faced many dangers along the central route. The weather and the terrain could be life threatening. Crossing the Sierra Nevada in winter, moving through a swift river, or traveling during rainstorms, a horse could easily throw its rider.

Traveling the central route offered many challenges, including rough terrain, raging rivers, and bad weather.

A Pony Express rider passes through Indian burial grounds.

However, the greatest danger came from American Indians. Along with many white miners, settlers, and businesses, the Pony Express was guilty of taking over Indian hunting grounds and using up their food sources. The Pony Express route ran through much Indian land.

American Indians fought back against the growing presence of the white man on their land by rising up against the Pony Express. During the Pyramid Lake War, the Paiute Indians battled white soldiers and burned Pony Express

American Indians attack a horseman from the Pony Express. No one knows for sure if Indians killed any Pony Express riders.

relay stations in Nevada and Utah. A number of the workers at these stations were killed. Though the fighting caused some delays in service, the Pony Express continued.

For all its successes, the Pony Express was short-lived. The express mail service stopped operating on October 24, 1861. It ended just eighteen months after its first run. It took until mid-November to finish delivering its mail.

This illustration shows people sending telegraphs from New York City in the 1860s.

Cross-country telegraph service had become available. The Pony Express was no longer the fastest way to send news across America. A few years later, the transcontinental, or cross-country, railroad was completed, further connecting the nation's East and West.

The U.S. transcontinental railroad was completed at Promontory Summit, Utah, on May 10, 1869.

Looking Back

The Pony Express was not a financial success. The COC & PP lost a great deal of money on the venture. However, the Pony Express helped the country in some important ways. Its successful runs proved that cross-country mail could be delivered all year using the central route.

This 1960 U.S. postage stamp celebrates the 100th anniversary of the start of the Pony Express.

The Pony Express was a vital link between the East and the West at the beginning of the Civil War. With the country splitting apart, communication between the two coasts became more important than ever.

In fact, it was during this time that the fastest Pony Express ride took place. In March 1861, President Abraham Lincoln's **inaugural address** was telegraphed to Fort Kearny, Nebraska Territory, from Washington, D.C. Then the Pony Express carried it to Folsom, California,

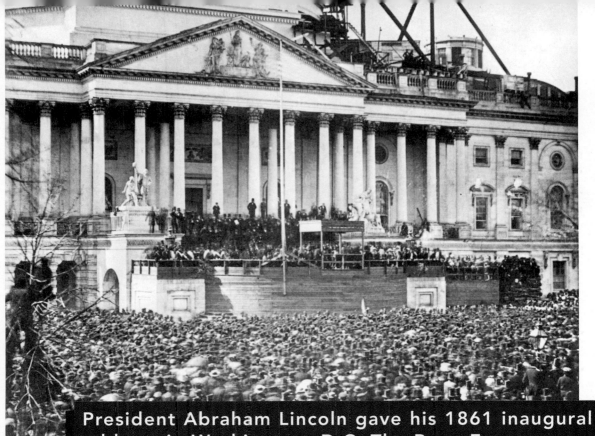

President Abraham Lincoln gave his 1861 inaugural address in Washington, D.C. The Pony Express, along with the telegraph, brought those words to Sacramento, California, in about a week.

where it was telegraphed to Sacramento. The entire trip took just seven days and seventeen hours.

The Pony Express earned its place in the nation's history. Despite its short life, the Pony Express has never been forgotten. Perhaps people have remembered it because it represented American spirit at its best. The riders had courage and a strong sense of duty. They proved that with hard work and determination, just about anything was possible.

THE PONY EXPRESS
ST. JOSEPH, MISSOURI

This statue in St. Joseph, Missouri, honors the spirit and strength of the riders of the Pony Express.

To Find Out More

Here are some additional resources to help you learn more about the Pony Express:

Books

DiCerto, Joseph. **The Pony Express: Hoofbeats in the Wilderness.** Franklin Watts, 1989.

Dolan, Edward F. **The Pony Express.** Benchmark Books, 2002.

Kroll, Steven. **Pony Express!** Scholastic, 1996.

Kule, Elaine A. **The U.S. Mail.** Enslow Publishers, 2002.

Quasha, Jennifer. **The Pony Express: Hands-On Projects About Early Communication.** PowerKids Press, 2003.

Savage, Jeff. **Pony Express Riders of the Wild West.** Enslow Publishers, 1995.

Wilson, Elijah Nicholas. **The White Indian Boy: The Story of Uncle Nick Among the Shoshones.** Paragon Press, 1991.

The Pony Express National Museum
914 Penn Street
St. Joseph, MO 64503
816-279-5059
http://www.ponyexpress. org/

Visit this museum and its site to get information about the Pony Express riders and their relay stations.

Pony Express National Historic Trail
http://www.nps.gov/poex/

The National Park Service has information about visiting historic trail sites. Be sure to click on the in-depth link for historical information about the Pony Express.

St. Joseph Museum
3406 Frederick Avenue
St. Joseph, MO 64508
816-232-8471
http://www.stjosephmuseum. org/

Visit this museum and its site to find out more about the history, route, and riders of the Pony Express.

Pony Express Home Station
http://www.xphomestation. com

Check out the Pony Express Schoolhouse, which has related maps and a quiz to test your knowledge.

Important Words

frontier the edge of a country

inaugural address a speech given by the president at the swearing in

mochila a leather saddlebag used to carry mail on horseback

Pony Express an express mail service that carried mail on horseback from St. Joseph, Missouri, to Sacramento, California

relay stations places at which Pony Express riders changed horses

routes roads or pathways used to get from one place to another

stagecoaches horse-drawn vehicles used in the past to carry people and mail

steamship a ship with a steam engine

telegraph a system of communication using electrical signals sent by wire

Index

(**Boldface** page numbers
  indicate illustrations.)

advertisements, **4,** 5–6
American Indians, 32–33, **32,
  34**
Bible, 26
California, 6, **10,** 11, 14, 40–41
Central Overland California
  and Pikes Peak Express
  Company (COC & PP), 12,
  14, 17, 24–25, 38
central route, **7, 9,** 14–15, 30,
  31, 33, 38
Civil War, 39–40
Colorado, 14
Folsom, California, 40
food, 22–23, 33
Fort Kearny, 40
Fry, Johnny, **16**
horses, 5, 6, **19, 21,** 22,
  24–25, 28, 30, **31**
Kansas, 14
land route, 12, **13**
letters, 8, 11, 12, 27, **28,** 29
Lincoln, Abraham, 40, **41**
mail service, 8, **10,** 11–12
map, **7**
Missouri, 6, 12, **17, 43**
mochilas (saddlebags), 29, **29**
Nebraska, 14

Nebraska Territory, 40
Nevada, 14, **19,** 35
Paiute Indians, 33, 35
Panama, **10,** 11
Pyramid Lake War, 33, 35
railroads, 12, 37, **37**
Red Rock Canyon, **9**
relay stations, 20, **21,** 22, 24,
  24, 35
riders, 6, 8, **16,** 20, **20,** 22–23,
  23, 25–26, **27,** 29, 30, **32,
  34,** 42, **43**
Sacramento, California, 6, 41
San Francisco, California, **10,** 11
sea route, **10,** 11
Sierra Nevada, 30
Simpson Springs Station, **24**
St. Joseph, Missouri, 6, 12,
  17, 43
stagecoaches, 12, **13**
stamps, **39**
steamships, **10,** 11
summer, 6, 26
telegraphs, 12, 36, **36,** 40, 41
transcontinental railroad, 37,
  37
Utah, 14, **24,** 35, **37**
Washington, D.C., 40, **41**
weather, 6, 15, **15,** 26, 30
winter, 15, **15,** 27, 30
Wyoming, **8,** 14

Meet the Author

Award-winning author Elaine Landau worked as a newspaper reporter, an editor, and a youth-services librarian before becoming a full-time writer. She has written more than 250 nonfiction books for young people, including True Books on dinosaurs, animals, countries, and food. Ms. Landau has a bachelor's degree in English and journalism from New York University as well as a master's degree in library and information science. She lives with her husband and son in Miami, Florida.